# BETTER BY SATURDAY™ PUTTING

*Books in the series*

# BETTER
# BY
# SATURDAY™
## PUTTING

Featuring Tips by
*GOLF MAGAZINE*®'s
## Top 100 Teachers
### with Dave Allen

**WARNER BOOKS**

NEW YORK    BOSTON

Warner Books

Time Warner Book Group
1271 Avenue of the Americas, New York, NY 10020
Visit our Web site at www.twbookmark.com.


Printed in the United States of America
First Printing: May 2004
10   9   8   7   6   5   4   3   2   1
Library of Congress Cataloging-in-Publication Data
Allen, Dave.
Better by Saturday—putting : featuring tips by Golf magazine's top 100 teachers
/ Dave Allen.
p. cm.
ISBN 0-446-53260-6
1. Putting (Golf) I. Title.
GV979.P8A46 2004
796.352'35—dc21   2003010751


Book design by HRoberts Design

# CONTENTS

# Foreword: Better by *When?*

When I heard the concept of this new series of books, "Better by Saturday," my reaction was immediate: "Hey, it's already Friday." But having seen the series, I'm convinced that the promise of its premise is fulfilled in these pages, which feature some of the best instruction you'll find in a month of Sundays.

If you're like many golf lovers I know, you dream of playing every day, try to play every week, and settle for a bit less than that. An occasional eighteen is better than nothing, but with so much time between rounds, it's tough to groove a swing. How can your muscles remember the inside-out path they took to the ball when you hit that huge drive your last time out? How can you hope to improve, knowing that PGA Tour pros pummel hundreds and even thousands of practice balls for every one you hit?

Here's how. This book contains the best, simplest tips we could get from the game's finest teaching pros, GOLF MAGAZINE's Top 100 Teachers. They work with thousands of ordinary golfers every week, as well as with top amateurs and Tour pros. They are the best in the business. And thanks to our

Top 100 Teachers, each of the four books in the Better by Saturday series—they cover driving; iron play and the long game; the short game; and putting—is full of advice that will help you play better your next time out. You don't have to change your swing. Just pay attention. It's easy, since these tips are clear and often entertaining. Even golfers who play every day will learn plenty.

It's all here: everything from teeing a ball up to hitting one off hardpan or out of a tough lie in a fairway bunker. If there's a situation or shot that always ruins your score, you'll find the cure in these pages. If your troubles take a new form every time out, you'll still find ways to shoot a lower score this weekend. And after that, you can re-read this volume for further improvement, or pick up another of our "Better by Saturday" books.

Imagine how good you might get by next month.

*Kevin Cook*
*Editor,* GOLF MAGAZINE

# Acknowledgments

Special thanks to Len Zamora and The Mirabel Golf Club in Scottsdale, Arizona, for allowing us the privilege to take these photographs on the spectacular Tom Fazio–designed championship course, located just down the road from Desert Mountain. A big thanks as well to our model for the putting and full swing books, Travis Fulton, an instructor with the PGA Tour Golf Academy at the World Golf Village in St. Augustine, Florida. Travis had to strike just about everything but the Heisman pose in our two days of shooting, and for that we're very appreciative.

Special thanks also go out to GOLF MAGAZINE photographer Fred Vuich, photographer Gary Newkirk, and GOLF MAGAZINE Associate Editor Greg Midland, without whom I'd have been lost in a sea of instruction tips and notebook paper.

Lastly, I'd like to thank GOLF MAGAZINE's Top 100 Teachers, an extremely talented group of instructors, many of whom I've had the great privilege of working with over the last five years. They've taught me so much about the game—probably too much—and for that, I'm extremely grateful—and resentful. Only kidding.—**Dave Allen**

# BETTER BY SATURDAY PUTTING

# Introduction

The night before he and Phil Mickelson staged their dramatic duel in the final round of the 1999 U.S. Open, the late Payne Stewart received some putting advice from his wife, Tracey. "You're moving your head," she told Payne. "Keep your head still."

Most average golfers are guilty of peeking every now and then on putts. But the best players in the world? Sure. And as Stewart stood over a 15-foot putt on the 72nd hole that would win the championship, it was his wife's tip that was foremost in his mind: "Keep your head still." Stewart never looked up until the ball was about two feet from the hole, and by then it was headed straight for the center of the cup, right into the record books.

One year later, it was another putting tip that carried Tiger Woods to victory at the U.S. Open. On Wednesday, the day before he would embark on his historic romp through Pebble Beach, Woods spent nearly two and a half hours on the practice green working on his stroke, and did it ever pay off! Woods failed to three-putt once over 72 holes, as he demolished the field by 15 strokes. All it took was a simple adjustment to his posture. "My hands were a little too low," said Woods. "I raised my hands up, which allowed me to release the blade down the line. From there, once I started making a few good strokes on the putting green, it kind of built up, and I putted beautifully."

That's the reality of putting. Everyone experiences their fair share of cold streaks, when the hole looks about the size of a dime. And yet, almost always, what pulls them out of their funk is something as subtle as their hand position, or their head movement. There's no need to overhaul the stroke, just find something simple that works for them—and fast—so by the time they tee off Saturday morning, their confidence on the greens is soaring once again.

On the pages that follow, we've compiled what we believe to be the greatest collection of putting tips, written by the finest collection of instructors ever—GOLF MAGAZINE's Top 100 Teachers. These tips were specifically chosen because of their simplicity; to help get you "Better by Saturday" without having to rebuild your stroke or think too much about the mechanics of your stroke. You'll find tips on how to handle breaking putts from noted short-game guru Dave Pelz, how to stabilize your left wrist from 2001 PGA Teacher of the Year Craig Shankland, and how to beat the yips from former PGA Club Professional champion Darrell Kestner. There's a whole chapter of tips devoted to helping you make more short putts—the kneeknockers—as well as some advice on how to read greens better and more efficiently.

Remember: No part of the game is more vital to your success than putting. Whether you break 80 or shoot 100, a good chunk of your strokes are going to occur on the green. Consider: When Tiger chewed up the field at Pebble, he averaged 27.5 putts per round, or 40 percent of the strokes he made that week. Forty percent! So, if you're struggling on the greens, we've got just the answers for you on the pages ahead.

# CHAPTER 1: THE SETUP

# Grip in the Palms

## *Place the handle between the heel and thumb pads*

Unlike the full-swing grip, which positions the club more in the fingers, the putting grip should place the handle in your palms, between the heel and thumb pad. This reduces the amount of wristiness in your stroke for more control and consistency.

Think of the putter grip as an extension of both arms. Held properly, the butt end should point on a line up your wrists and left forearm, ensuring that the putter is resting in the left palm. Add the right hand, being sure also to use the palm. Now you're lined up and ready to go. —***Todd Sones***

QUICK TIP

### Right Palm Faces Target

Good alignment boils down to the putterface angle, which is largely a function of a proper grip. Keep the back of the left hand and the palm of the right facing the target. This will position the right forearm directly behind the shaft, ensuring accuracy and stability. —*Bill Moretti*

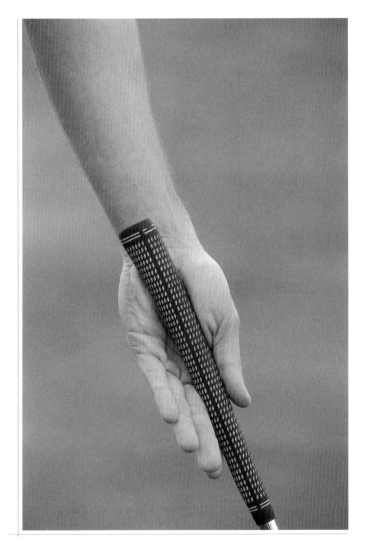

# Eye Position

*Use an old CD to place them slightly inside the target line*

The ideal putter path approaches the ball slightly from the inside, travels along the target line at impact, then returns to the inside on the follow-through, the same path for a full-swing shot. This creates optimal roll on the greens.

A perfect setup encourages the correct path. Make sure all your parts (feet, knees, hips, shoulders) are aligned square to the target line, especially your forearms. If the forearms are open or closed, they will directly affect the putter's path—and roll. Set your eyes one inch inside the target line [photo 1], not directly over it. To check this, place an old compact disc on the ground, shiny side up, and place the ball in the middle [photo 2]. Find your eyes in the reflection, and adjust your setup until they are where you want them. **—Dave Phillips**

# Distance from the Ball

*Drop a ball from your nose to see if your stance is just right*

A steady head position is vital to making solid contact. Any head movement during the stroke causes your body to move, which leads to mis-hits and poor distance control. Also, if you vary your head position from round to round, you'll distort your view of the putter-face, making it difficult to determine when it's square.

When my head position is correct, a ball dropped from the bridge of my nose will land on the back-inside corner of the ball I'm addressing [photos 1 and 2]. Try the same drill: You want the dropped ball to hit the inside half of the one on the ground or just inside of it. If it hits the outer half or falls way inside, you're standing too close or too far, respectively. Standing too close to the ball generally leads to a pull, whereas standing too far away tends to cause a push to the right. —*Darrell Kestner*

QUICK TIP

## Hands Below Shoulders

The position of your hands at address determines the shape of your putting stroke. To make a straight-back, straight-through stroke—the easiest to repeat because the putterface stays square to the target longer—your hands need to begin directly under your shoulders. —*Scott Sackett*

# The Claw

*Try this unusual grip to eliminate clubface twisting*

Struggling to find the hole with your conventional grip? Then you may want to try "the claw." It looks strange, but this unconventional grip helped transform Chris DiMarco into one of the top players on the PGA Tour.

Here's how to do it: First, take your normal left-hand grip, with the thumb extending down the top of the shaft. Turn your right hand so the back of it faces away from your body [photo 1], then bring it in from the side so the shaft pinches the skin between your thumb and forefinger [photo 2]. Rest the fore- and middle fingers on top of the shaft, with the ring finger and pinkie off to the side of the shaft.

During the stroke, the right hand is locked to the grip, eliminating the twisting that causes missed putts. The right arm has a lever action that works like a piston, back and forth, so it feels as if you're pushing the ball straight to the hole [photo 3]. In a conventional grip, the right hand twists and rotates during the stroke, altering the position of the clubface. —*John Redman*

# Perfect Posture

## *Position your thighs parallel to the puttershaft*

Focusing on your posture can improve your consistency and shave strokes. When your posture becomes too upright or too hunched over, it affects the path of the putter during the back-stroke: Unless the hands realign the clubface before impact, the putt will be pulled or pushed away from the target line.

Assume your address position so that the forearms form a virtually straight line with the puttershaft, and your thighs are parallel to the puttershaft. Align your shoulder joints, knees, and balls of your feet in a straight line, which positions your eyes slightly inside the target line. Once in this perfectly balanced setup position, the putter-head will travel along the correct inside-square-inside path throughout the stroke, without any manipulation by the hands. The result is a repeatable stroke and lower scores. —*Gregor Jamieson*

QUICK TIP

**Open Stance**

If you are in the habit of pushing putts to the right, set up to the ball with an open stance—with the left foot farther back from the target line than the right. Seeing the right foot in your peripheral vision dis-courages swinging the putter inside and promotes a straight-back, straight-through stroke. If the putterface stays aimed at the target, your chances of sinking the putt are pretty good. —*Rick Whitfield*

# Aiming Tool

*Start the ball on the proper line with the help of a marker*

If you don't take the time to precisely place your ball before every putt, you are wasting one of the best opportunities to shoot a lower score. On the green, the Rules of Golf allow you to mark your ball, clean it, and replace it any way you choose. The Rules also allow you to mark the ball so it is easier to aim.

Using a permanent marker, draw a line approximately one quarter of the way around the ball's circumference [photo 1]. This line is longer than the typical logo and is easier to use as an aid in squaring the putterface. From behind the ball—eyes looking down the target line—aim the stripe directly where you want the ball to start rolling; which, in the photo here, is four balls to the right [photo 2]. Once you have the stripe aimed, use the same routine before each putt to align the putter and your body to the line on the ball. Start by setting the center aim line on the putterhead behind the stripe on the ball [photo 3]. Next, align your stance line parallel to the stripe on the ball. Finally, align the rest of your body—hips, shoulders, and eyes—parallel to your stance line.

To be a great putter, you must be able to both start the ball on the proper line and create the proper speed. With a line ensuring proper aim, your mind can then focus fully on speed. *—John Gerring*

# CHAPTER 2: THE STROKE

# Firm Left Wrist

*Practice with a ball lodged between the grip and your wrist*

If you're having trouble hitting your putts on-line or making consistent contact, your left wrist may be breaking down during the stroke. If the left wrist doesn't remain frozen, the hands are free to flip the handle, which changes the loft and aim of the putterface. This typically leads to weak, glancing contact and poor distance control.

Use the following drill to stabilize your left wrist. Grip down about four inches with your left hand and lodge a ball between the grip and your left wrist [photo 1]. Then place your right hand on the grip and set up to the ball. Practice stroking putts with the lodged ball in place [photo 2]. If your left wrist breaks down, the ball will fall out. After several strokes, remove the ball and continue putting, retaining the feel of a stable left wrist. —***Craig Shankland***

*QUICK TIP*

## Move the Grip

To prevent the breakdown of the wrists, move the grip in the same direction as the putterhead. Wristiness comes when the grip moves in the opposite direction of the head. In short, make the grip an extension of the putterhead and pretend you're hitting the ball with it. This will keep your wrists firm and the putter on the right path. —*Todd Sones*

# Square Contact

### *Let the putterhead release past the handle*

Many amateurs make a pushing or blocking motion with their hands and arms, dragging the putterhead through, which prevents the head from releasing past the handle as it naturally does in a pendulum stroke. This stiff-wristed blocking motion may prevent the wrists from flipping through impact, but it also creates undue tension in the hands and wrists, reducing feel and consistency.

In a proper stroke, the hands and wrists respond to the weight of the swinging putterhead, allowing the putter to release as it swings through [photo 1]. The grip's butt end should point to your navel throughout the entire motion, especially after impact [photo 2]. When you allow the puttershaft to release like this on the throughstroke, the left arm stays close to the body and the putterface squares up and swings down the line. The result is a pure strike and a smooth roll. —*Kevin Walker*

QUICK TIP

## The Last Look

As you go through your normal preputt routine and take your final look at the hole, make sure to swivel your head so your eye line tracks directly over your intended target line; do not lift your head to look at the hole. This way, your head and shoulders don't move off the target line, which can change alignment and lead to inconsistent results. —*Donald Crawley*

# Right Wrist Angle

*Keep the angle intact to avoid breaking the left wrist*

You're not going to make all the six-foot putts you face (even the Tour pros miss roughly half of these kneeknockers), but you'll make more of these crucial scoring putts by eliminating left-wrist breakdown in your stroke. Under pressure, golfers stop the acceleration of the arms and shoulders before impact. The right hand applies the hit, forcing the left wrist to break down and send the ball off-line.

To eliminate this common flaw, focus on the angle formed between your right hand and wrist at address. Maintain this angle throughout the stroke, and you ensure the correct acceleration through impact. To get a feel for this, hit short putts in practice holding the putter with your right hand only [photos 1 and 2]. Be aware of the wrist angle and maintain it. You'll see that it forces the right arm and shoulder to control the throughstroke, so the left wrist stays firm and doesn't break down. —*Kip Puterbaugh*

# Forward Thinking

*Shorten the backstroke to ensure smooth acceleration at impact*

One of the most common putting faults with amateurs is taking the putter back too far and then having to decelerate through impact. This leads to inconsistent contact—it's hard to hit the ball solidly when you're steering the putterhead—and limits your feel for distance.

Here's a drill that will shorten your backstroke and help develop smooth acceleration through impact. Drop a ball about 25 feet from a hole, and place a second ball about eight inches directly behind the putterhead. (For fast greens, set the second ball an inch or two closer; for slow greens, move it back similarly.) Putt the first ball to the hole without touching the second ball [photo 1]. To reach the hole, you must accelerate the putter through impact [photo 2]. You'll start thinking less about the backstroke and more about the forward motion—the part that actually strokes the ball. *—Craig Bunker*

# Elbow Grease

*Keep the left elbow moving toward the target*

To keep the putterface square to the target line as long as possible, you need to keep the left elbow moving toward the target as you contact the ball. Many golfers keep this elbow tucked in against their side, both at address and throughout the stroke. This forces the right shoulder out toward the target line, making it extremely difficult to make square contact with the putterface.

To create some separation on your left side, adjust your setup so the left arm hangs away from your body, a bit closer to the target [photo 1]. To implement this change, place your hands slightly in front of the putterhead. Once your arms feel as if they're hanging from your shoulder sockets—instead of resting at your sides—you're ready to go.

From this setup, the arms will swing the putterhead along the target line longer [photo 2], keeping the putterface square and eliminating any need for manipulating the putterface. You'll consistently contact the ball in the middle of the putterface, making it far easier to judge distance and direction. *—Darrell Kestner*

# Topspin Roll

*Contact the ball with the lower half of the putterface*

The world's best putters have distinctly different styles, but the way they roll the ball is the same. Regardless of technique—left-hand low, belly style, or reverse overlap—great putters strike the ball with the middle to low part of the putterface, causing the ball to skid along the green for an instant, then roll with topspin. This helps the ball stay on its original line, a trait worth copying.

Learn to contact the ball with the middle to low part of the putterface by stacking five quarters a few inches behind the ball. Your goal is to swing the putter back and through without contacting the stack of quarters [photos 1 and 2]. Miss the stack, and you'll contact the ball with the lower half of the putterface, giving your putt the best chance to stay on-line and reach the hole.

Poor putters usually contact the ball high on the putterface with a descending stroke, driving the ball down into the green. The putt then pops into the air, causing the ball to bounce off its intended line. Putts hit this way usually finish short of the hole.

**—Mike Lopuszynski**

# No Peeking

*Stop your eyes from wandering with this drill*

In putting, solid contact is something most amateurs take for granted. You shouldn't: A 60-foot putt hit only half an inch off the sweetspot finishes five feet short. And you can chalk that miss up to distraction. Instead of focusing on the ball, most amateurs watch the putterhead go back to make sure it's straight, then, anxious to see what they've done, follow the ball to the hole immediately after contact. Those little eye and head movements are all it takes to throw the stroke off and make you miss the sweetspot.

Train yourself to stay focused by placing a ballmarker directly under the ball when you practice. Keep your eyes on the ball during the backstroke, and on the ballmarker after impact [photos 1 and 2]. Try to tunnel your vision this way on the course, too. **—*Kent Cayce***

QUICK TIP

## Pose the Finish

Just like in the full swing, a good finish position when you putt indicates that good things have led up to it. Keeping a light but constant grip pressure, hold your finish for a few seconds after you hit the putt, as if you're posing for a camera. This will simplify and smooth out your stroke. **—*Bill Moretti***

# Distance Control

*Concentrate more on the pace of the stroke*

It should take the same amount of time to make a stroke that rolls the ball three feet as it does to roll it 60 feet. The difference is the pace of the stroke: A 60 footer requires a longer stroke at a faster pace; a three footer requires a shorter stroke at a slower pace. Finding the right pace is essential to controlling how far your putts roll.

After reading the putt (uphill, downhill, left-to-right, etc.), determine its speed—do you want to die the ball into the hole or ram it in? Then take one or two practice strokes, each time the same length back and through at the pace you plan to use for the actual stroke. The practice stroke tells the muscles how much energy is required to reach the target and thereby helps formulate a pace for the stroke. After your final practice stroke, take one final look to confirm your feel for the distance, trust your instincts, and go. **—Mike McGetrick**

# Forward Press

### *Keep your hands ahead of the putterhead*

Few shots are more mentally demanding than the five-foot knee-knocker to save par or halve a hole. One way to eliminate the pressure is to stop leaving yourself in "choke range," which means making better approach putts. To do that, you need to make flush contact with the ball.

The key is to make sure the butt end of the grip is even with or slightly ahead of the ball at impact. If you allow the grip to lag behind, the bottom of the putterface will catch the ball on the upswing. This adversely affects contact and adds loft to the face, and thus reduces roll.

At address, set the butt even or slightly ahead of the ball, the way you want it at impact. Many Tour players initiate their stroke by pressing their hands slightly toward the target. This forward press acts like the waggle in the full swing, helping to relieve tension and jump-start the stroke. Just as important, it serves as a reminder that your hands need to be in front of the putterface at impact. **—Paul Trittler**

# CHAPTER 3: SPEED PUTTS

# Breaking Putts

*Double the break and add two to the heart*

The majority of missed putts—around 80 percent—miss on the low side, below the hole (referred to as the "amateur side"). That's because most golfers under-read the break; they see only one-quarter to one-third of the actual break, with their subconscious adjusting both the setup and stroke to compensate for the rest.

To make more breaking putts, start by doubling the break you see. Say you read a putt as breaking six inches. That's six inches from the edge, plus another two inches to the heart of the cup. Double your initial read to 12 inches, then add two inches from the edge to the middle of the hole, so your new read is for 14 inches of break.

There's no need to get hung up on inches or exact distances. Estimate. See the high point of the break, figure roughly twice that, add a little more (the edge-to-middle distance), and aim at this new high point. Then make a straight, unmanipulated stroke.

**—*Dave Pelz***

# Left-to-Right Breakers

*Position the ball farther forward in your stance*

For most right-handed golfers, the putt that breaks to the right [photo 1] is especially difficult because the putt moves away from the body. The tendency is to under-read the break and miss on the low side of the hole.

To sink more left-to-right putts, adjust your ball position to counteract the slope, as you do with a full swing from an uneven lie. Choose the starting line and then move the ball forward in your stance, from inside the left heel to opposite the big toe [photo 2]. This gives the putterface more time to square up and helps start the putt on the correct line instead of off to the right. Reverse the concept on right-to-left putts, moving the ball back to about the middle of your stance. —*J. D. Turner*

QUICK TIP

### Finish 17 Inches Past the Cup

There is only one optimum speed for putts, that which rolls the ball 17 inches past the hole if it misses. Whenever you imagine a putt, see the ball rolling at a speed that will make it finish 17 inches past the cup. Once you know where to start the ball for that read, forget the break and focus on a stroke that will produce that speed. —*Dave Pelz*

# Pressure Putts

### *Sink more by pretending there are two targets*

To help you sink more pressure putts, pick out two targets: an intermediate target and a second target at the back of the hole. You could choose a blade of grass, a brown spot, etc. The intermediate target should be at the apex of the break, where the ball begins to fall toward the hole. The second target helps you gauge the putt's speed: How hard must you hit it to reach the back of the hole? Aim your putterface at the intermediate target, commit to it, then focus on speed.

Another helpful tip on up- and downhill putts is to visualize the putt's speed and match your stroke to it. Determine the number of seconds you think it will take for the ball to reach the hole; if it's four seconds, rehearse a stroke that will produce a four-second roll, taking into account how the slope may affect the speed. **—Rob Akins**

# Two-Tiered Greens

### *Play to an imaginary cup short or past the hole*

Successfully putting on multilevel greens depends on the proper use of energy. Rolling putts up or down a tier, your ball loses or gains energy, so putts roll shorter or longer than you would expect from the length of the stroke.

To compensate for these energy gains or losses, first estimate the size of the elevation change. Usually it's a few inches, but I've seen drops and rises of a foot or more—as much as six feet! Once you have a rough idea of a tier's size, it's a simple matter of multiplying. Going uphill, multiply the elevation change by 10, then imagine that the hole you're putting to is that far past the real hole [photo 1]. So if the tier is two to three inches high, your "target" is two feet past the real hole (two and a half inches times 10 equals 25 inches, or roughly two feet). Then make a stroke strong enough to get the ball to this new target.

Putting downhill, the same principle applies, but in the opposite direction. Do the math, then set your imaginary cup that far short of the real hole [photo 2]. So for a three-inch-high tier, your new target is 30 inches short of the hole. Focus your mind's eye on the imaginary target, then use the touch you'd employ on a normal, flat green. **—*Dave Pelz***

# Slick Downhillers

### *Grip down to the shaft to soften the blow*

While it's true that hitting a putt away from the face's center transfers less energy to the ball, it's also true that hitting it on the toe causes the putterhead to twist—if only slightly—making it hard to start the putt on-line.

If you want to hit the ball with less force, grip down on the putter. Set your left hand slightly below the middle of the grip and your right hand at the bottom, almost touching the shaft. With this method, regardless of the stroke's length, you'll transfer less energy to the ball. You can make contact on the putter's sweetspot, giving it the best shot at staying on-line. **—Rick Grayson**

QUICK TIP

### Let All Putts Die

On all putts, even a two-foot tap-in, let them die in the hole, feeding the ball slowly so it falls in gently. The dying putt has a few advantages over putts that charge the hole: It's more likely to drop in the side door; there's no worry of hitting through the break; the ball rarely rolls so far past that there's a chance of three-putting; and short putts almost never lip out. *—Jim Flick*

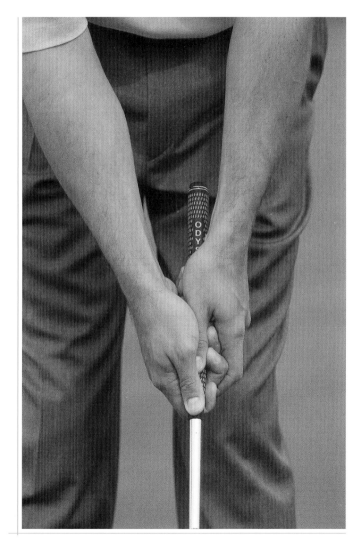

# CHAPTER 4: SHORT PUTTS

# Focus on the Process

*Forget the outcome and stroke firmly through the ball*

Every miss in golf offers the hope of a miraculous recovery—except the short putt. Standing over a three footer, you know full well that a miss will mean a stroke you'll never get back, that whatever happens for the rest of the day, your score should be at least one shot lower. This sense of finality breeds frustration and jittery nerves.

Remind yourself that you can't make a putt, you can only make a stroke. In other words, focus on the process instead of the outcome. Avoid the tendency to steer or guide the putter on short putts; stroke firmly through the ball. Payne Stewart used to pick a spot an inch in front of the ball [photo 1], make that his hard focus, and then stroke through that spot [photo 2]. For him, it took the pressure off of making perfect impact. And don't try to be too precise with your aim, as that only adds to the tension. Envision a path to the hole as wide as the cup; keep the ball within that path and the putt will drop. —*Dr. Richard Coop*

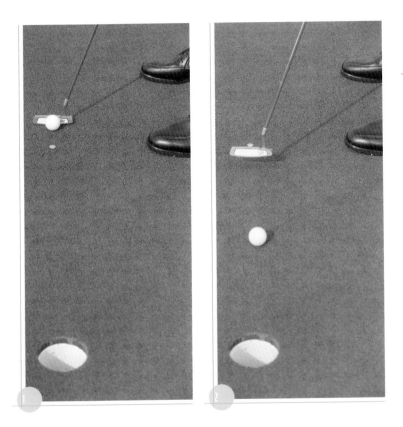

# Kick the Yips

### *Hit your shoe and stop to gain a feel for a firm strike*

All "yippers" share a common trait: fear of missing short putts. This fear causes the smaller muscles in the hands and wrists to twitch uncontrollably and flip the putter through impact, causing very poor contact.

If you've got a case of the yips, try this drill: Take your normal putting setup, then extend your left leg so the ball of your left foot is just ahead of the actual ball. Then lift the toes of your left foot so the ball can roll under your shoe [photo 1], and make your normal putting stroke. The shaft will hit your shoe and stop, but the ball will continue toward the hole [photo 2].

As the shaft hits your shoe, notice that your wrists remain firm. There's no wrist collapse, no wobble in the stroke. Repeat this drill several times to gain the feel for a firm left wrist, a solid stroke, and a straight roll. —*Darrell Kestner*

QUICK TIP

**Trust Your Ears**

On short putts, let your ears be your eyes. Keep your eyes down and listen for the sound of the ball falling into the cup. It will keep your body still and your stroke on-line. —*Bruce Hamilton*

# Head Movement

*To stop looking up prematurely, look up*

Stop yourself from looking up prematurely on short putts by looking up *before* you start. Set up as you normally do, then tilt your head in order to fix your eyes on the hole (or along your intended line) just before taking the putter back. As long as you're set up well, you should have no trouble striking the ball purely. This not only makes it impossible to pull up during the stroke, but looking at your target also sharpens your sense for how hard you have to hit the ball. —*Craig Shankland*

QUICK TIP

### Push the Putterhead to the Hole

Acceleration through impact is everything! Forget the ball and concentrate on pushing the blade through to your target. You'll stop decelerating the putter and start hitting the ball firmly into the back of the hole. —*Dick Tiddy*

# Sloping Putts

*Cheat toward the toe or heel*

You have a six-foot putt that breaks from right to left and slopes like Mount Kilimanjaro. The object is to hit the ball hard enough to hold the line, but not so firm that you could face a 10 footer coming back. What do you do?

Aim above the hole, as you normally would to play the break. Address the ball off the toe of the putter [photo 1], then make your normal stroke. Don't worry about the exact point of impact: If it's off the toe, the ball will start well right and take a big break because it didn't receive much power. Hitting closer to the sweetspot means less starting-line error, but more energy. The two "errors" will counteract each other, giving your putt a chance of falling in.

For short, left-to-right-breaking putts, position the ball more toward the heel [photo 2]. Again, making contact closer to the heel means more break and less energy. **—*Dave Pelz***

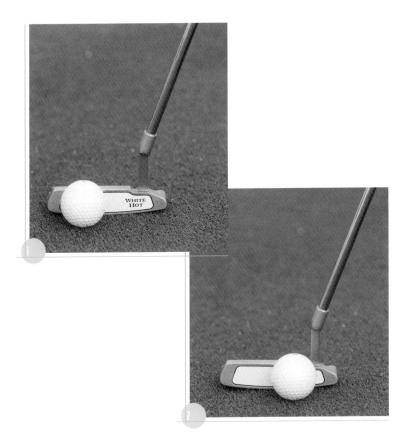

# Straight Method

*Build a practice station to groove a straight-back, straight-through stroke*

Successful short putting demands good alignment—your feet parallel to the target line and your putterface moving back and forth perpendicular to that line. Groove the ideal setup by using your three longest irons and your putter.

Place two long irons parallel to each other and aimed at the hole, creating a corridor slightly wider than your putterhead. Set the ball between the shafts, then use your putter grip to help place the third iron, which will mark your stance line. The standard putter grip is 11 inches long, and I recommend standing about 10 inches away from the ball; so place the butt end of the putter's grip one inch past the inside shaft, and the third iron at the bottom of the grip and parallel to the other clubs [photo 1]. Now you're ready to practice a straight-back, straight-through putting stroke that travels along the target line [photo 2]. Soon, you'll start seeing more short putts drop into the hole. —*Fred Griffin*

# Forward Stroke

### *Lower the putter to keep hands, arms relaxed*

Why do amateurs miss so many short putts? They try to accelerate too much on the forward stroke, which leads to tension and, in turn, opens or closes the putterface, sending the putt off-line.

Here's a great drill to correct this. Set up a track for the putter-head on your practice green using two shafts. Practice stroking putts within the track and—here's the key—slowly lower the putterhead to the ground at the completion of each stroke. Your hands and arms must be relaxed to do this—and, once the putterhead is set down, you can see if the face is square. —*Jim Flick*

QUICK TIP

### Left Shoulder up, Ball in Cup

Missed short putts are often caused by turning the shoulders in a rotary motion (around the spine) instead of rocking them up and down like a seesaw. A true pendulum stroke dictates that the putterhead rise and fall with the shoulder motion. Remember this rhyme: Left shoulder up, ball in cup; left shoulder around, ball above ground. —*Martin Hall*

# CHAPTER 5: LONG PUTTS

# Putt like You Chip

## *Use your chipping grip and swing for more power*

I've noticed time and again that golfers leave lag putts short much more often than they roll them past the cup. One reason is that the golfer doesn't make a long enough backstroke on long putts, and then tries to make up for it with a late "hit" from the hands and wrists.

To encourage a longer backswing, try my "Chipputt" method. Simply put, it's making a chip shot swing with your putter. Stand tall, as you do when chipping; this improves your distance perception and gives you a better view of the line [photo 1]. Split the difference between your normal back-in-the-stance chipping position and your forward-in-the-stance putting position. Finally, use your chipping grip and chipping swing [photo 2]. The putter will strike the ball at the bottom of your swing arc, and your habit of leaving these putts short will disappear as a result of your more powerful chipping swing. —*Dave Pelz*

QUICK TIP

### Blindfold Test

To test your feel for distance, close your eyes, walk to where you think the hole is, and try to drop the ball in it. At first, you'll be surprised how far off you are. As you get better at this drill, your feel for speed will improve, too. —*Bruce Hamilton*

# Body Movement

*Allow your weight to shift slightly from side to side*

It's helpful to stay completely still on short putts, where the line is the key to holing out and feel is not a major concern. However, on putts of 30 feet or longer, you'll make a better stroke and gain a better feel for distance by letting your weight shift slightly from side to side. This shift should be virtually imperceptible, but you should feel your body weight shift slightly to the right on the backstroke [photo 1] and onto your left side on the forward stroke [photo 2]. This will allow you to make a free-flowing stroke with consistent rhythm.

If you try to keep your weight rock-steady on longer putts, you will instinctively apply more power with your hands and wrists on your way through the ball, resulting in a loss of speed and putterface direction. Remember, being a little shifty on longer putts will provide maximum control. **—*Rick Grayson***

QUICK TIP

### Get Down in Two

Outside of 24 feet, your only objective should be two-putting rather than three-putting. Forget the kind of precision alignment used for shorter putts, and aim to leave your ball inside a five-foot-diameter circle around the hole. *—Rick Whitfield*

# Hook Putt

*Swing the putterhead on an arc, not straight back and through*

When he won the 1997 Masters, Tiger Woods didn't have a single three-putt on the treacherous Augusta National greens. He repeated the feat in 2000 at Pebble Beach to win the U.S. Open. For us mere mortals, however, just going an entire round without a three-putt would be something. The secret, of course, is getting your first putt close.

On the really long ones, swing the putterhead on an arc [photos 1 and 2]—as if you were trying to hook the putt—not straight back and through, which creates a steep angle of descent into the ball.

It also helps to stand taller on longer putts, gripping a half-inch higher on the putter. This allows you to extend your arms, creating more wrist hinge during the stroke and more momentum for the putterhead. —*Mitchell Spearman*

# Hinge and Hold

### *Shorten the stroke and hold the hinge for more power*

Standing over a long putt, most golfers worry more about the length of the stroke than making solid contact. As a result, the backstroke is usually too long, which leads to a decelerating forward stroke and a putt that comes up well short of the hole.

To create a shorter, more powerful stroke that discourages deceleration, try the "hinge-and-hold" method. Start by tightening your stomach muscles and gripping the ground with both feet for maximum stability. Also, set your weight slightly forward and point your elbows to your hips.

Make a short backstroke by rocking your shoulders and hinging both wrists slightly [photo 1]. This will move the putterhead behind your hands, creating more leverage and power. On the forward stroke, hold the hinge as your shoulders rock toward the target, and let the putterhead accelerate through impact. If the back of your left wrist faces the target [photo 2], you've made solid contact. **—*Patti McGowan***

# CHAPTER 6: GREEN READING

# Follow the Flow

### *Determine the break by where the water drains*

Every green is designed to let rainwater run off, so once you determine the direction that the water will drain, you'll have a good idea of the putt's overall break. Imagine tossing a bucket of water at the hole [photo 1], picturing how it would flow toward the hole. This is the general break your putt will follow.

Some other things to consider: As you repair your ballmark, check the firmness of the green [photo 2]. If the green is hard, expect a faster roll; if the green needs major repair work, the green is soft and you can expect a slower roll. Remember: the faster the green, the more the putt will break.

Another thing that affects the putt's speed is the grain, which is the direction the grass grows. Bermudagrass, which is generally found in the South and other warm climates, has very pronounced, easy-to-read grain; bentgrass, found on greens in the North, is finer and harder to read. In general, if the grass looks shiny; it's lying down (downgrain) and you can expect a faster putt. If it's dark green, you will be putting into the grain, so expect a slower putt. **—*Paul Trittler***

# Important Footsteps

*Walk the line to the hole and back to gauge the terrain*

People who think they're plumb-bobbing don't really know what they're doing. They're just holding the clubshaft in front of them and guessing at how the putt will break. In addition, making a correct read of the terrain while plumb-bobbing doesn't factor in the speed of the green, which dictates the amount of break in any putt.

Instead, walk along the line to the hole and back [photo 1] to get a feel for the terrain—uphill, downhill, and/or sidehill. Also, remember that the final few feet before the hole are the most critical, because as the ball slows down, the break will be its greatest. So make sure to view the putt from behind the hole as well [photo 2]. Once you've gauged these factors, you can marry the effort required to the break you feel and see. These steps will provide a more accurate read than dangling a putter ever will. —*Rick Grayson*

QUICK TIP

### Be Road Wary

How you read break depends largely on the kind of greens you're used to playing. If you come from fast, undulating greens, you'll tend to over-read putts when you get to flatter ones. If you play flat greens, you'll generally under-read breaks when you play away. Keep this in mind and adjust accordingly. —*Dr. Richard Coop*

# Long Putts

*Take a walk on the lower side*

The best perspective for reading a long putt is halfway along the line on the low side. Assessing the putt from the halfway point gives you a good feel for the overall distance, and the low side reveals any rise or fall. Keep in mind, distance is the key on long putts. Reading putts from behind the ball is more important from short range, where the break should be your primary concern. —*Jim Flick*

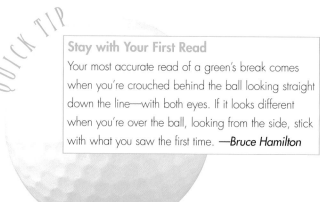

QUICK TIP

**Stay with Your First Read**

Your most accurate read of a green's break comes when you're crouched behind the ball looking straight down the line—with both eyes. If it looks different when you're over the ball, looking from the side, stick with what you saw the first time. —*Bruce Hamilton*

# CHAPTER 7: PRACTICE

# Scoring Putts

### *Start putting in a horseshoe fashion, "around the world"*

Short, "scoring" putts make for tedious practice, so try this game, a derivation of one you might have played on the basketball court.

Place eight to 10 tees in a horseshoe pattern with about two or three feet between each tee and the hole at the open end. Start putting at the end of the horseshoe, which should be about two feet from the hole. After you make the first putt, go to the next tee. The object is to move all the way "around the world" without missing. It may take a while, but when you finally make every putt, you'll have great confidence with the flatstick.

**—Dick Farley**

# Speed and Line

*Roll putts every few feet along the break line*

The most important part of putting is visualizing what the ball has to do to go in the hole. Forget about stroke mechanics for a minute and find a 20 footer on your practice green with at least a few feet of break. Hit the putt several times to get the read, then place balls directly on the break line every few feet, from the cup to the 20-foot mark.

Putt in the ball nearest the hole, then the next one, and so on, rolling each ball over the spots held by the closer balls. To use the full break, try to roll each putt over the front lip. In the process, you'll learn to aim at intermediate targets along the line and will develop an understanding of how speed determines line.

**—Jim Flick**

# Keep It Square

*Use the "Rake Drill" to get a feel for a square putterface*

Simply put, if the putterface isn't square, the ball won't roll on-line. You must be able to feel the putterface position at all times. The Rake Drill will help. Starting with a straight four-foot putt, take your normal address. Then, instead of making a backstroke, simply push the ball toward the hole [photos 1, 2, and 3]. This will immediately show you whether the putterface is square. Once you're comfortable from four feet, move back to six, and eventually to eight. The constant repetition trains you to extend the putterhead down the target line on the follow-through while maintaining a square face. **—*Kent Cayce***

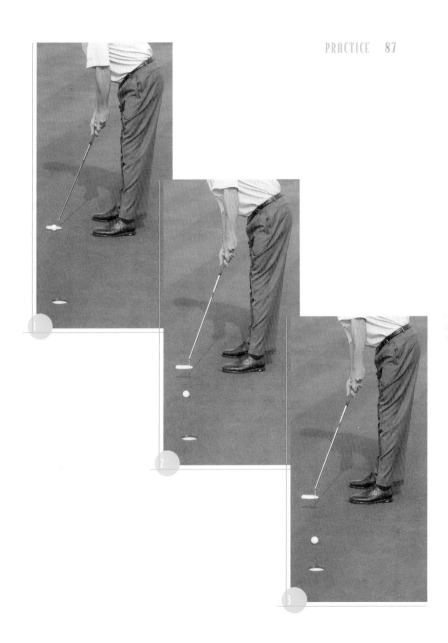

# Breaking Putts

*Eliminate the amateur side, below the hole*

The key to breaking putts is keeping the ball above the cup—on the pro side—so it can roll in on the high side. Because most players don't start breaking putts high enough, they miss low, below the hole, which has come to be known as the amateur side.

You must rule the low side out of the picture when lining up a breaking putt. For example, if you face a 10-foot putt that breaks left to right, your target should be the left two-thirds of the cup. The right third is "no-man's-land." Practice by sticking a tee in front of no-man's-land, and putting so your ball stays above the tee. This drill teaches you what it takes to make breaking putts by focusing your concentration and narrowing the target.

**—Dick Farley**

# In the Zone

*Sharpen your distance control by putting just past the hole*

On the practice green, stick a tee in the ground a putter-length behind the hole [photo 1]. From 10 feet away, putt three balls to the hole. Then gradually increase your distance from the hole and repeat. Your goal is to put enough pace on the ball to make the putt, but if you miss, you want the ball to finish past the hole but short of the tee [photo 2]. As you improve, gradually reduce the size of your target zone behind the hole to sharpen your distance control. —*Mike McGetrick*

QUICK TIP

### How Good a Lag Putter Are You?

Take three balls to the putting green. Stand at one edge of the green, putt one ball to each of the three holes farthest away from you, and measure the lengths of the second putts left to hole out. Write these three second-putt lengths on a scorecard and repeat the test twice more from completely different edges of the green. Add all the second-putt distances together and divide by nine. The longer your average second putt, the more likely you are to three-putt. —*Dave Pelz*

# Keep a Steady Head

*Press your head against a golf cart to build a reliable stroke*

Train your head and body to remain still through the stroke by practicing with your head against a wall or golf cart. This position allows you to feel a stroke completely controlled by the arms and shoulders.

There should be no motion from the waist down on short putts, and your head should stay steady throughout. Feel the forearms controlling the stroke as they swing under the shoulders. At the completion of the stroke, the right palm faces the same direction as the clubface, and the wrists have not hinged from their original address position: This keeps clubface aim consistent during the stroke. **—Darrell Kestner**

# Arms and Mostly Shoulders

*Wedge a club under your armpits to get the shoulders rocking*

Control about 80 percent of the stroke with the shoulders, the rest with the arms. A good way to feel this motion is to putt with another club wedged under both armpits.

To practice path, place a club on the target line, turn your putter upside down, and set up so the end of the grip points directly at the club on the ground. Keep the shaft pointing at the target line throughout the stroke. When you do this, the putter-head will move up and inside the target line on both the backswing and throughswing. This will keep the shaft on plane, which produces the correct path—just like in the full swing.

**—Dave Phillips**

For more golf tips, as well as news, travel advice, equipment updates, and more, visit **GOLF MAGAZINE** on the web at www.golfonline.com.